The Best Meals are made from the

Best Recipes!

MEAL PLANNER RECIPES EDITION

@ Journals & Notebooks

Meal Planner

	Breakfast	Lunch	Dinner
Monday			
Tuesday			
Wednesday			
Thursaday			
Friday			
Saturday			
Sunday			

	Breakfast	Lunch	Dinner
Monday			
Tuesday			
Wednesday			
Thursaday			
Friday			
Saturday			
Sunday			

	Breakfast	Lunch	Dinner
Monday			
Tuesday			
Wednesday			
Thursaday			
Friday			
Saturday			
Sunday			

Meal Planner

	Breakfast	Lunch	Dinner
Monday			
Tuesday			
Wednesday			
Thursaday			
Friday			
Saturday			
Sunday			

Notes

	Breakfast	Lunch	Dinner
Monday			
Tuesday			
Wednesday			
Thursaday			
Friday			
Saturday			
Sunday			

Meal Planner

	Breakfast	Lunch	Dinner
Monday			
Tuesday			
Wednesday			
Thursaday			
Friday			
Saturday			
Sunday			

notes

	Breakfast	Lunch	Dinner
Monday			
Tuesday			
Wednesday			
Thursaday			
Friday			
Saturday			
Sunday			

Meal Planner

	Breakfast	Lunch	Dinner
Monday			
Tuesday			
Wednesday			
Thursaday			
Friday			
Saturday			
Sunday			

notes

	Breakfast	Lunch	Dinner
Monday			
Tuesday			
Wednesday			
Thursaday			
Friday			
Saturday			
Sunday			

	Breakfast	Lunch	Dinner
Monday			
Tuesday			
Wednesday			
Thursaday			
Friday			
Saturday			
Sunday			

	Breakfast	Lunch	Dinner
Monday			
Tuesday			
Wednesday			
Thursaday			
Friday			
Saturday			
Sunday			

Meal Planner

	Breakfast	Lunch	Dinner
Monday			
Tuesday			
Wednesday			
Thursaday			
Friday			
Saturday			
Sunday			

NOTES

	Breakfast	Lunch	Dinner
Monday			
Tuesday			
Wednesday			
Thursaday			
Friday			
Saturday			
Sunday			

	Breakfast	Lunch	Dinner
Monday			
Tuesday			
Wednesday			
Thursaday			
Friday			
Saturday			
Sunday			

	Breakfast	Lunch	Dinner
Monday			
Tuesday			
Wednesday			
Thursaday			
Friday			
Saturday			
Sunday			

Meal Planner

	Breakfast	Lunch	Dinner
Monday			
Tuesday			
Wednesday			
Thursaday			
Friday			
Saturday			
Sunday			

notes

	Breakfast	Lunch	Dinner
Monday			
Tuesday			
Wednesday			
Thursaday			
Friday			
Saturday			
Sunday			

Meal Planner

	Breakfast	Lunch	Dinner
Monday			
Tuesday			
Wednesday			
Thursaday			
Friday			
Saturday			
Sunday			

notes

	Breakfast	Lunch	Dinner
Monday			
Tuesday			
Wednesday			
Thursaday			
Friday			
Saturday			
Sunday			

Meal Planner

	Breakfast	Lunch	Dinner
Monday			
Tuesday			
Wednesday			
Thursaday			
Friday			
Saturday			
Sunday			

notes

	Breakfast	Lunch	Dinner
Monday			
Tuesday			
Wednesday			
Thursaday			
Friday			
Saturday			
Sunday			

	Breakfast	Lunch	Dinner
Monday			
Tuesday			
Wednesday			
Thursaday			
Friday			
Saturday			
Sunday			

	Breakfast	Lunch	Dinner
Monday			
Tuesday			
Wednesday			
Thursaday			
Friday			
Saturday			
Sunday			

Meal Planner

	Breakfast	Lunch	Dinner
Monday			
Tuesday			
Wednesday			
Thursaday			
Friday			
Saturday			
Sunday			

NOTES

	Breakfast	Lunch	Dinner
Monday			
Tuesday			
Wednesday			
Thursaday			
Friday			
Saturday			
Sunday			

Meal Planner

	Breakfast	Lunch	Dinner
Monday			
Tuesday			
Wednesday			
Thursaday			
Friday			
Saturday			
Sunday			

notes

Meal Planner

	Breakfast	Lunch	Dinner
Monday			
Tuesday			
Wednesday			
Thursaday			
Friday			
Saturday			
Sunday			

Notes

Meal Planner

	Breakfast	Lunch	Dinner
Monday			
Tuesday			
Wednesday			
Thursaday			
Friday			
Saturday			
Sunday			

	Breakfast	Lunch	Dinner
Monday			
Tuesday			
Wednesday			
Thursaday			
Friday			
Saturday			
Sunday			

Meal Planner

	Breakfast	Lunch	Dinner
Monday			
Tuesday			
Wednesday			
Thursaday			
Friday			
Saturday			
Sunday			

Notes

Meal Planner

	Breakfast	Lunch	Dinner
Monday			
Tuesday			
Wednesday			
Thursaday			
Friday			
Saturday			
Sunday			

notes

Meal Planner

	Breakfast	Lunch	Dinner
Monday			
Tuesday			
Wednesday			
Thursaday			
Friday			
Saturday			
Sunday			

	Breakfast	Lunch	Dinner
Monday			
Tuesday			
Wednesday			
Thursaday			
Friday			
Saturday			
Sunday			

Meal Planner

	Breakfast	Lunch	Dinner
Monday			
Tuesday			
Wednesday			
Thursaday			
Friday			
Saturday			
Sunday			

Notes

	Breakfast	Lunch	Dinner
Monday			
Tuesday			
Wednesday			
Thursaday			
Friday			
Saturday			
Sunday			

	Breakfast	Lunch	Dinner
Monday			
Tuesday			
Wednesday			
Thursaday			
Friday			
Saturday			
Sunday			

	Breakfast	Lunch	Dinner
Monday			
Tuesday			
Wednesday			
Thursaday			
Friday			
Saturday			
Sunday			

	Breakfast	Lunch	Dinner
Monday			
Tuesday			
Wednesday			
Thursaday			
Friday			
Saturday			
Sunday			

	Breakfast	Lunch	Dinner
Monday			
Tuesday			
Wednesday			
Thursaday			
Friday			
Saturday			
Sunday			

Meal Planner

	Breakfast	Lunch	Dinner
Monday			
Tuesday			
Wednesday			
Thursaday			
Friday			
Saturday			
Sunday			

notes

	Breakfast	Lunch	Dinner
Monday			
Tuesday			
Wednesday			
Thursaday			
Friday			
Saturday			
Sunday			

	Breakfast	Lunch	Dinner
Monday			
Tuesday			
Wednesday			
Thursaday			
Friday			
Saturday			
Sunday			

	Breakfast	Lunch	Dinner
Monday			
Tuesday			
Wednesday			
Thursaday			
Friday			
Saturday			
Sunday			

Meal Planner

	Breakfast	Lunch	Dinner
Monday			
Tuesday			
Wednesday			
Thursaday			
Friday			
Saturday			
Sunday			

NOTES

Meal Planner

	Breakfast	Lunch	Dinner
Monday			
Tuesday			
Wednesday			
Thursaday			
Friday			
Saturday			
Sunday			

	Breakfast	Lunch	Dinner
Monday			
Tuesday			
Wednesday			
Thursaday			
Friday			
Saturday			
Sunday			

	Breakfast	Lunch	Dinner
Monday			
Tuesday			
Wednesday			
Thursaday			
Friday			
Saturday			
Sunday			

	Breakfast	Lunch	Dinner
Monday			
Tuesday			
Wednesday			
Thursaday			
Friday			
Saturday			
Sunday			

	Breakfast	Lunch	Dinner
Monday			
Tuesday			
Wednesday			
Thursaday			
Friday			
Saturday			
Sunday			

	Breakfast	Lunch	Dinner
Monday			
Tuesday			
Wednesday			
Thursaday			
Friday			
Saturday			
Sunday			

	Breakfast	Lunch	Dinner
Monday			
Tuesday			
Wednesday			
Thursaday			
Friday			
Saturday			
Sunday			

Meal Planner

	Breakfast	Lunch	Dinner
Monday			
Tuesday			
Wednesday			
Thursaday			
Friday			
Saturday			
Sunday			

notes

	Breakfast	Lunch	Dinner
Monday			
Tuesday			
Wednesday			
Thursaday			
Friday			
Saturday			
Sunday			

	Breakfast	Lunch	Dinner
Monday			
Tuesday			
Wednesday			
Thursaday			
Friday			
Saturday			
Sunday			

	Breakfast	Lunch	Dinner
Monday			
Tuesday			
Wednesday			
Thursaday			
Friday			
Saturday			
Sunday			

	Breakfast	Lunch	Dinner
Monday			
Tuesday			
Wednesday			
Thursaday			
Friday			
Saturday			
Sunday			

	Breakfast	Lunch	Dinner
Monday			
Tuesday			
Wednesday			
Thursaday			
Friday			
Saturday			
Sunday			

	Breakfast	Lunch	Dinner
Monday			
Tuesday			
Wednesday			
Thursaday			
Friday			
Saturday			
Sunday			

	Breakfast	Lunch	Dinner
Monday			
Tuesday			
Wednesday			
Thursaday			
Friday			
Saturday			
Sunday			

Meal Planner

	Breakfast	Lunch	Dinner
Monday			
Tuesday			
Wednesday			
Thursaday			
Friday			
Saturday			
Sunday			

NOTES

	Breakfast	Lunch	Dinner
Monday			
Tuesday			
Wednesday			
Thursaday			
Friday			
Saturday			
Sunday			

	Breakfast	Lunch	Dinner
Monday			
Tuesday			
Wednesday			
Thursaday			
Friday			
Saturday			
Sunday			

Meal Planner

	Breakfast	Lunch	Dinner
Monday			
Tuesday			
Wednesday			
Thursaday			
Friday			
Saturday			
Sunday			

Notes

Meal Planner

	Breakfast	Lunch	Dinner
Monday			
Tuesday			
Wednesday			
Thursaday			
Friday			
Saturday			
Sunday			

Notes

	Breakfast	Lunch	Dinner
Monday			
Tuesday			
Wednesday			
Thursaday			
Friday			
Saturday			
Sunday			

	Breakfast	Lunch	Dinner
Monday			
Tuesday			
Wednesday			
Thursaday			
Friday			
Saturday			
Sunday			

	Breakfast	Lunch	Dinner
Monday			
Tuesday			
Wednesday			
Thursaday			
Friday			
Saturday			
Sunday			

Meal Planner

	Breakfast	Lunch	Dinner
Monday			
Tuesday			
Wednesday			
Thursaday			
Friday			
Saturday			
Sunday			

notes

	Breakfast	Lunch	Dinner
Monday			
Tuesday			
Wednesday			
Thursaday			
Friday			
Saturday			
Sunday			

	Breakfast	Lunch	Dinner
Monday			
Tuesday			
Wednesday			
Thursaday			
Friday			
Saturday			
Sunday			

ingredients

preparation

procedure

ingredients

preparation

procedure

ingredients

preparation

procedure

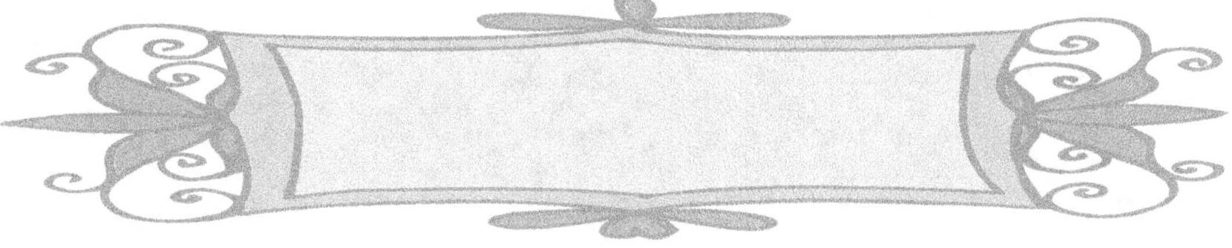

ingredients

preparation

procedure

ingredients

preparation

procedure

ingredients

preparation

procedure

ingredients

preparation

procedure

ingredients

preparation

procedure

ingredients

preparation

procedure

ingredients

preparation

procedure

ingredients

preparation

procedure

ingredients

preparation

procedure

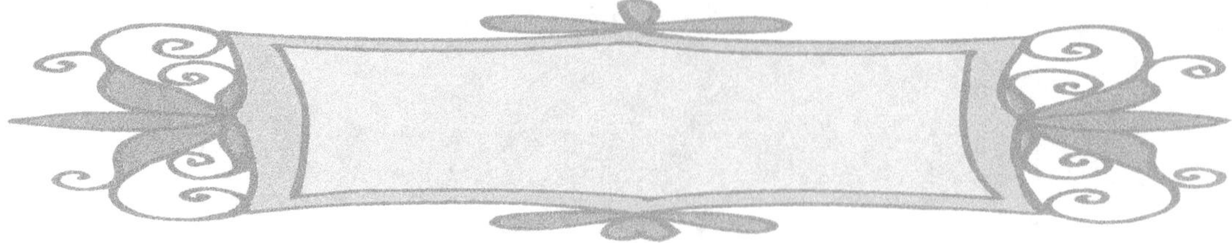

ingredients

preparation

procedure

ingredients

preparation

procedure

ingredients

preparation

procedure

ingredients

preparation

____

procedure

ingredients

preparation

procedure

ingredients

preparation

procedure

ingredients

preparation

procedure

ingredients

preparation

procedure

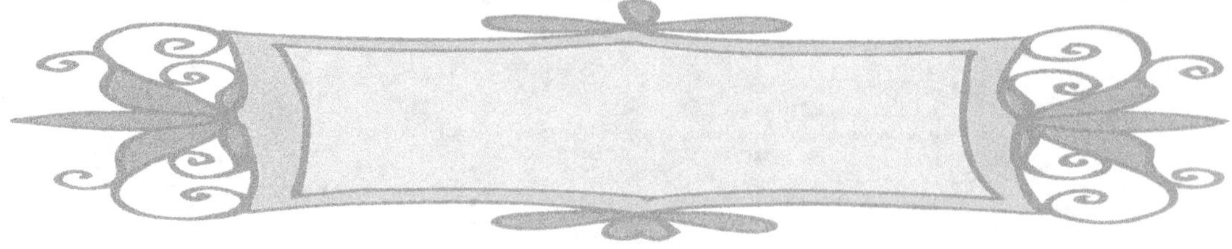

ingredients

preparation

procedure

ingredients

preparation

procedure

ingredients

preparation

procedure

ingredients

preparation

procedure

ingredients

preparation

procedure

ingredients

preparation

procedure

ingredients

preparation

procedure

ingredients

preparation

procedure

ingredients

preparation

procedure

ingredients

preparation

procedure

ingredients

preparation

procedure

ingredients

preparation

procedure

ingredients

preparation

procedure

ingredients

preparation

**procedure